Ready Steady Go!

Planning the Move from Primary to Secondary School

A Workbook for Children with Special Educational Needs and their Parents.

Dr Alison Doyle

Published by Caerus Education
Dublin
Ireland
www.caerus.ie

ISBN 978-1-5272-0514-7

About the Author

As a teacher, psychologist, and researcher, my work has taken me to schools, colleges, and universities all over the world, and as a parent of three children, I have navigated many school types and systems. Currently, I live and practice in Dublin, supporting children and young adults to manage school transitions. I'm also lucky enough to get out and about, speaking at conferences and providing workshops to parent and community support groups. I have also published *Planning Transitions for Young People with Special Needs and Disabilities: A Practical Workbook for Students and Parents.*
www.caerus.ie

About the Illustrator

I was born in 1985 in Waterford, and currently live in Dublin. My passion for drawing and illustration started at a young age, inspired by 'The Simpsons'. I graduated from Ballyfermot College, Dublin in 2013, with a Diploma in Illustration. As a freelance Illustrator, my usual medium is hand-draw pen and ink, and my commissioned works have included portraits, murals for two primary schools, print media, and personalised mementoes for weddings and other events. I'm also working on an illustrated autobiography, *The Life of Ray Watson,* which depicts key moments in my life.
www.facebook.com/IllustratoRay

Acknowledgements

Sincere thanks to the families and professionals across Ireland who piloted and evaluated earlier versions of this workbook, and in particular to the Trainor family, Catherine Walsh, and Fiona Murtagh.

Introduction

Ready, Steady, Go! Is a practical resource for parents and children, to support the move from primary to secondary school. It is designed to be used as a shared workbook that combines advice and checklists for parents, with activities for children that will help them to prepare for their new school. It is especially useful for children who experience stress or anxiety, who have difficulty with changes in routine or managing new environments, and who may require more focused support and structured forward planning. The themes and activities are designed to build confidence around managing change, to develop coping strategies, and to familiarise young people with the differences between primary and secondary school. The content has been written for use by the widest range of young people as possible, therefore, not all of the activities may be relevant to all children or parents.

Saying farewell to the primary years and stepping through the doorway to adolescence is a complex, challenging, and exciting time for young people and their parents. There are significant changes in the teaching and learning environment, the curriculum, and social behaviour. Some young people require emotional, behavioural, and academic support to manage such changes, and so a transition plan should be discussed and implemented well before the conclusion of primary school. Plan early and plan well is the key to successful transition outcomes.

This workbook is a response to requests from families and support groups, for structured guidance and planning for children approaching the end of primary school. I believe it will also be of interest to practitioners working with young people and their families, such as support teachers, special needs assistants, and therapists. *Ready, Steady, Go!* is a companion to *Planning Transitions for Young People with Special Needs and Disabilities*, a programme of support for parents and students focused upon the move from secondary or high school, to college, university, or employment.

What are the challenges?

1. Children are understandably anxious about getting to know and managing a larger and more complex environment, teaching styles and subjects. There are different routines and structures to the school day, and engagement with peers and teachers in the classroom is more formal. A greater level of independence is required.

2. The dynamics of social relationships in secondary school are quite different to those of primary school as children approach the onset of adolescence. Current frendships may not be transferred to a new school meaning that your child must forge new friendships and manage a greater number of social circles.

3. The focus of learning shifts from the acquisition of baseline academic skills, for example, learning to read, to intensive use of these skills across a broader curriculm – reading to learn.

Using this Workbook

The most important help you can give to your child is confidence, security, and encouragement. It is important that you prepare your son or daughter for differences and changes well in advance of starting in a new school. A gradual introduction using the experiences of near and extended family, is a good way to do this.

Plan. You should plan for this transition from the beginning of the last year in primary or elementary school. You will need to work with the Special Needs Co-ordinator or Organiser, and staff in both the primary and secondary school. You will also need to gather and organise paperwork and formal documentation.

Talk. Encourage your son or daughter to talk about people, roles, and routines in their current school, and to think about how these might contrast with their new school. They will have concerns that they may not have verbalised, but which might cause underlying stress and anxiety. Talking might include the use of discussion, video modelling, social stories, role play, and dialogues.

Act. A great deal of the stress and anxiety – for both parents and students - can be alleviated by engaging in activities which provide you with knowledge and confidence. The process of searching for information, completing an activity, and crossing it off a checklist, provides a sense of achievement and forward movement.

What's in the Workbook?

The workbook content has been written for use by parents and students, however, it can also be usefully implemented by professionals supporting students in their transition. It is very important that the workbook is used as a shared experience, and that tasks and activities for both adults and children are viewed as a part of transition planning. You should begin and continue to work on this activity book together, and encourage other family members to take an interest in the content.

You can photocopy pages from the student section of this workbook. It's a good idea to set aside a regular time to work on the activities together, but it is also important not to force this, or to be too rigid about timings.

Part 1: A Plan for Parents

Finding Out provides parents and carers with a set of checklists for organising meetings and visits, and gathering information and paperwork connected to managing:

- School environment
- Safety and social relationships
- Academic tasks including homework
- Transitions and routines
- Personal belongings

Let's Talk About.... The transition to secondary school coincides with the onset of adolescence, a period of significant emotional, physiological, and psychological changes. Additionally, the change in educational context impacts upon friendships, social groups, environments, and methods of teaching and learning. Initiating and maintaining conversations about these changes may be difficult but is necessary, and this section provides guidance on topics and beginning these conversations with your child.

Supporting Communication looks at the challenges of managing social and academic communication within the school environment, particularly for students who experience difficulties with receptive and expressive language. This section provides suggestions and tools to support the development of effective communication with peers and adults in school.

Coping Strategies provides activities and tools that will assist your son or daughter to develop strategies for managing potentially stressful situations within the school environment. These might include changes to routines, transitions between classes, or sensory overload.

Managing the School Part of School is a significant task for both parents and students, particularly during the first year of secondary school. This section provides guidance on managing the practical aspects of school-based learning, including managing homework, and maintaining high quality communication between home and school staff.

Individual Transition Plans should be completed by the young person, their parents, and support professionals. Some young people may have an Individual Education Plan which also sets out these requirements. Where this is not available or does not exist, the Individual Transition Plan fulfills the same function. The Individual Transition Plan template ensures that strengths, challenges, and needs are communicated to school staff prior to the move from primary school.

Part 2: Getting to Know My New School

This part of the workbook is completed by your child, and comprises three sections:

Finding Out sets out a number of activities which will help your child to discover concrete information about their new school. They provide opportunities to engage in meaningful conversations to address anxieties, and indicate areas for further discussion or action. The exercises in this section build knowledge and confidence about how secondary school works.

Getting Organised and Managing Time focuses on time management, and organising personal belongings. This includes getting to grips with lockers, timetables, and homework.

Talking About Changes mirrors the section from the parent workbook and is intended to be used simultaneously. This section begins with an activity that provides an opportunity for parents and students to talk about worries or concerns, and to develop coping strategies for a range of scenarios, such as managing the environment, homework, routines and rules, and meeting new teachers.

Taking Care of Myself includes activities for developing skills, identifying and using 'safe spaces', and creating tools and coping mechanisms for use within the learning and social environment. It also includes sections on personal care, making friends, and managing tricky situations.

All About Me encourages students to produce a personal profile to give to staff in secondary school.

Part 1: A Plan for Parents

Finding Out

Let's Talk About....

Supporting Communication

Coping Strategies

Managing the School Part of School

Individual Transition Plans

Finding Out

Choosing the right secondary school for your son or daughter is such an important decision. 'Which school would you recommend?' is probably the question I get asked the most. Unfortunately, sometimes the ethos and culture of a school can fluctuate with a change in head teacher or a school board. Because recommendations from friends or professionals can be tricky, this section of the workbook provides you with a toolkit to discover important information about a prospective school.

We begin with sets of key questions that can help you to decide whether a school is right for your child. Asking these questions will also give you an opportunity to explore the atmosphere and environment of the school, and to find out more about the people who will be supporting your son or daughter. Requesting a visit during school hours is a very important part of getting a feel for the school. It isn't necessary to ask or answer all the questions provided on the following pages, but they will help you to think about important aspects of school life. There is a space provided to make notes.

The second part provides you with a set of core checklists. These are designed to help you source the information and paperwork that is needed for the beginning of the new school year, and to assist you with making arrangements for how your child is supported in school, and by whom. The checklists cover the following topics or themes:

1. Learning about the school context
2. Safety and social relationships
3. Managing school work
4. Managing transitions and school routines

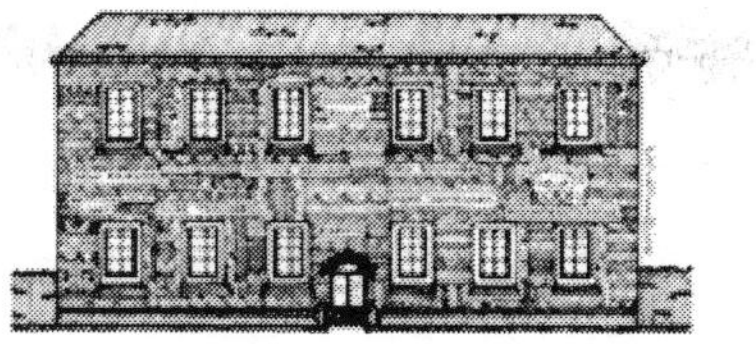

About the school

- ☐ How close is the school to your house?
- ☐ How long will it take you to get there in the morning / afternoon / in an emergency?
- ☐ Will it be possible for your son or daughter to travel there independently (eventually)?
- ☐ How big is the campus?
- ☐ Is the atmosphere friendly and inviting?
- ☐ Is the building run down or does it look well cared for?
- ☐ Do you get a sense of the personality of the school?
- ☐ How many floors are there? Is the building on one level and are there ramps?
- ☐ Is it a site with many different buildings to navigate?
- ☐ Is it fully accessible? Is it well sign-posted?
- ☐ Is the surrounding area noisy?
- ☐ What are the noise levels like at busy times of the day?
- ☐ Where is the recreation area? Where do students go at break time?
- ☐ How secure is the site?
- ☐ Is there a feeling of calmness and orderliness of movement around the school?
- ☐ Are there quiet rooms for the pupils to use?
- ☐ Are the classrooms organised in a traditional way, or is it more communal? Are there a lot of open plan areas?
- ☐ How many bathrooms are there? Are they clean? How many hand dryers do they have? Are they noisy? Is there an accessible toilet?

Notes

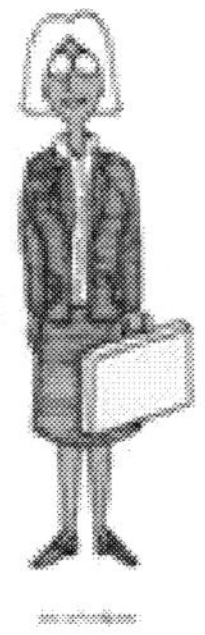

About the people

- ☐ Do key staff have a good understanding of special educational needs and disability?
- ☐ Are they trained and / or qualified in this area of knowledge?
- ☐ How long have teaching staff been in the school?
- ☐ Have they shown interest in finding out more about the needs of your son or daughter?
- ☐ How many support staff would be available?
- ☐ Are ancillary and office staff friendly?
- ☐ How interested does the receiving teacher or Year Head seem?
- ☐ How many staff are on duty at break or lunch times?
- ☐ Is there a rota or are there specific staff for these times?
- ☐ Where is the staff room and is it easy to find?
- ☐ Will your child know anyone else moving to this school?
- ☐ Is it connected to the primary school?
- ☐ What is the general demeanour and behaviour of students arriving and leaving?
- ☐ What is the average class size / ratio to teaching staff?
- ☐ What are the learning support facilities like?

Notes

School organisation and management

- [ ] How does the school communicate with parents?
- [ ] Are comprehensive resources provided on the school website?
- [ ] How often do parent / teacher meetings take place?
- [ ] Does the school use student support plans or student profiles?
- [ ] Is there an active parent - teacher association?
- [ ] Does the school or its students regularly win awards?
- [ ] Is the work of students visible in the school?
- [ ] Is a newsletter produced each term or school year?
- [ ] How many community events is the school involved in?
- [ ] Does classroom activity appear to be well organised and managed?
- [ ] Are school policies and rules readily available?
- [ ] What arrangements are made for students who are unable to engage with aspects of the curriculum, for example, Physical Education or the Games period?
- [ ] Is there a quiet area or respite room where students may take time out?
- [ ] Is there a school nurse or other person available to students at all times i.e. not part-time or timetabled to be elsewhere?
- [ ] How is the end of the lesson signalled: bell or siren?
- [ ] Is a loudspeaker system used?
- [ ] Is there a sign-in system for students who are late? Is there a reward / sanction system?
- [ ] How are classes and year groups organized?
- [ ] Are parents welcomed into the school? What activities are arranged for parents? Do the things that you are told take place in the school, actually happen?

Notes

Navigating the learning environment

- ☐ How many rooms will your child need to transition to during the day?
- ☐ Is there a buddy system?
- ☐ Where do students eat?
- ☐ How does lunchtime work?
- ☐ Where do PE lessons take place, and where do students change clothes?
- ☐ Are there lockers available and how do these work?
- ☐ Is there a locker area close to the staff room?
- ☐ If your child needs a place to calm down or be alone, is there a place to go? Is this allowed?
- ☐ How flexible is the school on facilitating sensory processing difficulties?
- ☐ Is the school open to use of technology for learning e.g. iPad and laptops?
- ☐ Does the school use interactive whiteboards or blackboards?
- ☐ Are students encouraged to use digital textbooks?
- ☐ Are there clear boundaries and rules during recreation periods?
- ☐ Is the school secure?
- ☐ What measures are in place to ensure that students do not leave the school premises?
- ☐ Are there lunchtime and after-school activities?
- ☐ Do these provide for a wide range of interests?

Notes

In this section I have provided a set of checklists of tasks and actions for each of the key areas associated with successful transitions: learning about the school context, safety, and social relationships, managing school work, and managing transitions and school routines.

You should start this checklist at the beginning of the final year in primary school. That might sound like a long way into the future, but many of these tasks take time, particularly those that involve people from outside of the family.

Use the checklists to think about the information you need to gather, and the tasks you need to complete, before your son or daughter makes the move from primary to secondary school. Of course, you may not need to do all of these things, in which case you should place a mark in the 'Not Applicable' (N/A) box. The checklists are a visual guide to help you to keep track of outstanding tasks that need to be completed before the move to secondary school, for example:

Managing homework tasks	**Working on it**	**Done**	**N/A**
Set up a study area at home. Include study aids such as a whiteboard or noticeboard.			
Provide a set of colour coded storage boxes / folders for each subject.			
Make a book and equipment list for each subject that can be 'check listed'.			
Make a book and equipment list for each school day that can be 'check listed'.			
Add timetable, homework and tasks to organising and planning software.			

Record your progress in one or more of the three columns. Place a mark in the 'Working on it' box if this is in progress, and check this task off in the 'Done' box when complete.

Learning about the school environment	**Working on it**	**Done**	**N/A**
Meet with Special Educational Needs Co-ordinator or Organiser.			
Meet with School Principal.			
Meet with Year Head.			
Meet with Class Teacher.			
Meet with Special Needs Assistant.			
Meet with learning support and resource teachers.			
Agree and arrange a series of familiarisation visits over the year.			
Identify important rooms / spaces in school.			
Collect photographs of school buildings / classrooms.			
Ask for a map / floorplan of the school.			
Discuss solutions to potential sensory overload areas, in particular:			
• Bathrooms and eating areas			
• Communication systems: loudspeakers, bells and sirens			

Safety and social relationships	Working on it	Done	N/A
Ask about a ‘safe place’ or time-out room.			
Ask about key ‘go to’ people.			
Agree on a procedure or protocol for using ‘safe place’ or ‘go to’ strategies.			
Agree on a communication cue for permission to leave the classroom.			
Identify an alternative place to eat lunch.			
Identify an alternative bathroom.			
Talk about potential areas of difficulty:			
• Classroom and lesson / activity transitions.			
• Break and lunch times.			
• Talking to peers.			
• Bullying and peer pressure.			
• Asking for help.			
• Asking and responding to questions in class.			
• Getting changed for sports / PE.			

Managing school work	**Working on it**	**Done**	**N/A**
Communication method between home and school e.g. journal, homework diary, or online messaging?			
Agree on an initial modified homework load e.g. an essential minimum.			
Agree on acceptable homework format e.g. use of computer.			
Managing transitions and routines	**Working on it**	**Done**	**N/A**
Communication between home and school e.g. journal, homework diary, or online messaging.			
Agree on an initial modified homework load e.g. an essential minimum.			
Agree on acceptable homework format e.g. use of computer.			
Confirm key times and routines associated with the school day.			
Identify acceptable alternatives to break arrangements e.g. use of Library or safe place.			
Identify the breaks and transitions throughout each school day.			
Create a visual timetable for each school day.			
Create visual cue cards for 'now', 'next' and 'later'.			
Create visual cue cards for each school day.			
Create visual communication cards for common or anticipate scenarios.			

Let's Talk About....

Young people experience many changes when moving to secondary school. It is useful to begin talking about these differences during the last year of primary education, however, it is not recommended that you overwhelm your son or daughter by introducing these topics all at once, or addressing them repeatedly. Where they crop up in conversation naturally or are instigated by your young person, take advantage of this opportunity. Social stories are helpful for introducing routines and structures, and comic strip conversations can assist with visualising situations. These techniques were developed by Carol Gray, and both print and digital resources based on this approach, are widely available.

Some children will benefit from a relaxed, conversational approach, others may prefer facts and details. You know the best and most appropriate way of beginning these conversations with your son or daughter, but it is important to be accurate, clear, and consistent in your explanation of how things are going to happen in secondary school. Therefore, you need to ensure that you are armed with ALL of the relevant information before beginning a conversation or working on a social story, so you will need to complete the checklist activities first.

Step 1: Encourage your son / daughter to talk about their current school in terms of likes and dislikes, friendships, staff, break times, what they are good at, what they may have found difficult initially, how difficulties were resolved. It is also a good opportunity to discuss situations or aspects of the school or social environment that they have learned to manage, and how they did this. Talk about how their experience of primary school has changed over time.

Step 2: Link these experiences to moving to a new school, and how they might be similar or different. Introduce your own family stories about the transition to secondary school. Look at photographs or home videos, and encourage grandparents, cousins, and older siblings to share their memories and to provide examples of overcoming difficult situations.

Step 3: Gradually introduce the topics suggested in the next two pages. You may want to record the outcome of these conversations, or any actions that need to be taken, for example:

- 'will need to discuss with the class teacher'
- 'ask for this to be added to the IEP / SNA responsibilities'
- 'to practice with mum or dad'
- 'needs social story or role play'

In some cases, schools must apply for additional teaching and special needs resourcing in advance of the beginning of the school year. There may be a specific timeframe for this application and you should check this with your education provider or government department. For this reason, it is important that you discuss the support needs that your son or daughter will require in secondary / high school, before the end of their final year in primary / elementary education.

Topic	**Outcome or action**
Remembering my schoolbooks and equipment	
What to do at break / lunch time	
Learning new subjects	
Managing the homework	
Remembering school rules	
Meeting my new teacher	
Understanding the lessons	
Organising my school things	
Coping with sounds and noise levels	

Topic	Outcome or action
Making new friends	
Getting changed for sport / PE	
Having a different uniform	
Finding my way around school	
Traveling to and from school	
Starting conversations	
Moving between classrooms	
Using the bathrooms	
Remembering the names of teachers	
Using a locker	

Using social stories

Social Stories™ are based on the premise that instructions to comply with rules or social behaviour, are not effective if the rationale for doing so, does not make sense. Because social rules or social cues are quite specific to the person, place, situation or event, there are billions of potential combinations of meanings and outcomes. Therefore, the way in which we teach everyday skills, must be unique to the learner and their personal goals.

A personalised social story should share information in a way that is completely accessible to the learner, and which enables them to make their own understanding of a skill, task, activity, context, or situation. Examples can be found at:

1. **TASN Autism and Tertiary Behavior Supports** website from the Kansas State Department of Education's Special Education Services. They have a collection of stories or social narratives for all age groups in Word, Powerpoint and pdf.

2. **Special Education Technology (SET)** in British Columbia also provide templates for stories and storyboards.

3. **The Watson Institute** resource bank.

4. **Carol Gray's Social Stories** website and 15th anniversary edition of her publication.

You can write your own stories for use with iPad or Android tablets, however, it is just as easy to type, word process or handwrite these, and to illustrate them using EasyRead graphics and icons that are freely available on the web. Writing a social story takes a lot of preparation, practice, editing and revision, but you will be writing unique stories that are specific to the needs of your child, and that makes all the difference. You can personalise the stories with family detail or anecdotes. Here is the beginning of a social story that can be developed to incorporate the structure of the school day:

Going to Secondary School

On Monday 1st September, I will be going to a new school which is called Parkside Community School. I will leave the house with Mum at 8.00 a.m. and we will drive to my new school which is on Green Road. We will arrive at approximately 8.30 a.m. As it is the first day back to school for everyone in The City, there may be a lot of traffic, so it is difficult to predict the exact time that we will arrive. When we arrive at school Mum will come into school with me. We are going to meet my SNA who is called Catherine. She is the person who will be helping me during class. Then my Mum will leave. She will come back to pick me up at 4.30 p.m. I will wait for her outside the school office.

Lessons begin at 9.00 a.m. The first lesson will be in my home classroom G4 with my new class teacher who is called Mr Wilson. G4 is on the ground floor of the school. I will go to class with Catherine and we are going to sit at the back of the classroom in the left-hand corner by the window. Mr Wilson will take the register to check who has arrived in school. He will then talk to us about the timetable and school rules. If I don't understand I need to tell Catherine.

Supporting Communication

One of the greatest challenges for teachers in post-primary school, is getting to know large numbers of students that they may only teach once or twice a week. Determining what students are thinking and how they are feeling whilst delivering the content of the lesson, can be tricky. Using non-verbal signals are an excellent method for managing actions in a busy secondary classroom. If these are pre-agreed or pre-arranged with teachers at the beginning of the year, they can significantly reduce anxiety levels.

Hand signals are not unusual, they are used frequently in many aspects of life, for example, by traffic policemen, by the military, and in sport. Students raise their hands numerous times during a lesson, therefore using a hand signal or sign is unlikely to attract undue attention. In many primary school classrooms, students and teachers use signs to communicate certain expectations or actions such as bathroom breaks, "quiet" signals, and silent congratulations or 'well done' moments.

The simplest strategy is to assign meaning to each of the 1 to 5 hand signs. These can be substituted for requests or statements suited to the post-primary school environment.

For example:

0 fingers = don't feel well

1 finger = bathroom break

2 fingers = office / school nurse

3 fingers = need to move

4 fingers = need help

5 fingers = have a question

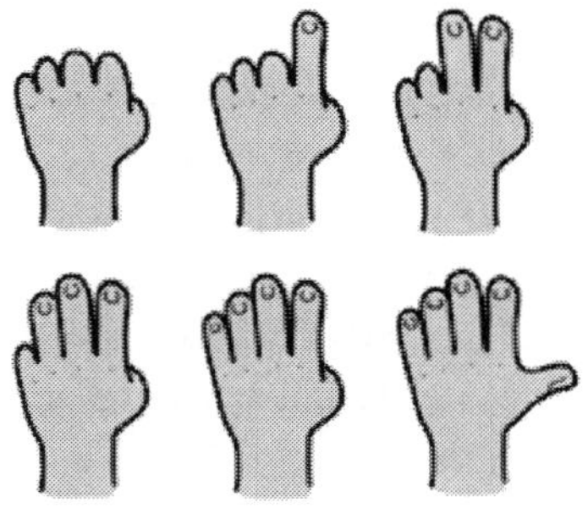

Alternatively, you may decide to use non-verbal signals that your student and his or her teachers may previously have used as a communication tool. The Special Needs or Learning Support Assistant, learning support teacher, and pastoral care teacher such as a Guidance Counsellor, can be instrumental in ensuring that all teachers follow through with this strategy.

Communication cards

A set of small laminated cards may be useful to help with managing communication. This is a useful support as your son or daughter will need to communicate with many more adults in secondary school, including teachers and administrative and ancillary staff. Where appropriate, these can gradually be phased out as confidence and familiarity increases. You should discuss the need for these as part of the 'Let's talk about...' activity in the preceding section. Ideally, they should provide a combination of a symbol / picture and a written caption.

It is important to limit the number and subject matter of cards to those which are necessary to prevent misconceptions or misunderstandings, and to reduce stress and anxiety. Their purpose is not to remove the necessity for spoken communication, and in fact doing so may be counter-productive.

Communication cards permit school staff and your child to communicate in a way that is not disruptive to other students, or demeaning or embarrassing for them. They are especially helpful in situations where a student feels overwhelmed or emotional. Student cards may include pictures, facial expressions or text that communicates feelings, statements, or questions such as:

- I feel upset and anxious
- I don't understand
- I'm not sure what to do or where to go
- May I leave the room?

Teacher cards might include:

- You are doing well
- Lesson has finished, pack away your things
- Do you need help?

The need for the student to use communication cards should be included in the IEP or Transition Plan, and must be communicated to all members of the school community who will be working with your student. If you are not confident about making your own materials at home, pre-printed cards for social communication, facial expressions and school activities are widely available from SEN / disability support groups. If you are working with a Speech and Language Therapist or Occupational Therapist, they may be able to provide you with similar resources.

Communication cards or fans are easy to make using materials from any good stationery or office supply shop.

You can use the templates on the next page, and illustrate the card using you own drawings or images from magazines. You can also download and use symbols from organisations such as Easy on the Eye.

OR

Buy a set of blank playing cards from a craft shop, illustrate and laminate these before punching a hole in the corner, and securing with a keyring circlet.

Making communication cards is a good opportunity to talk to your children about the way in which students and teachers interact in secondary school, and how this might be different from primary school.

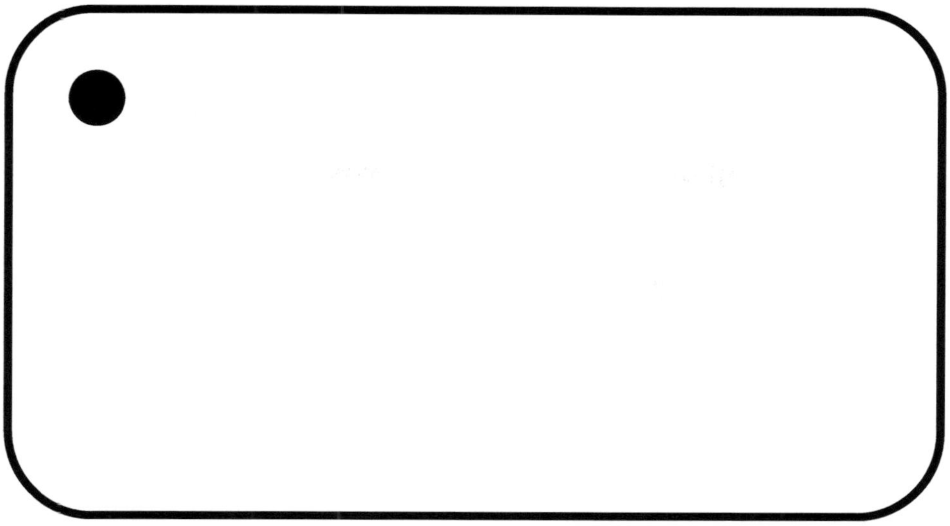

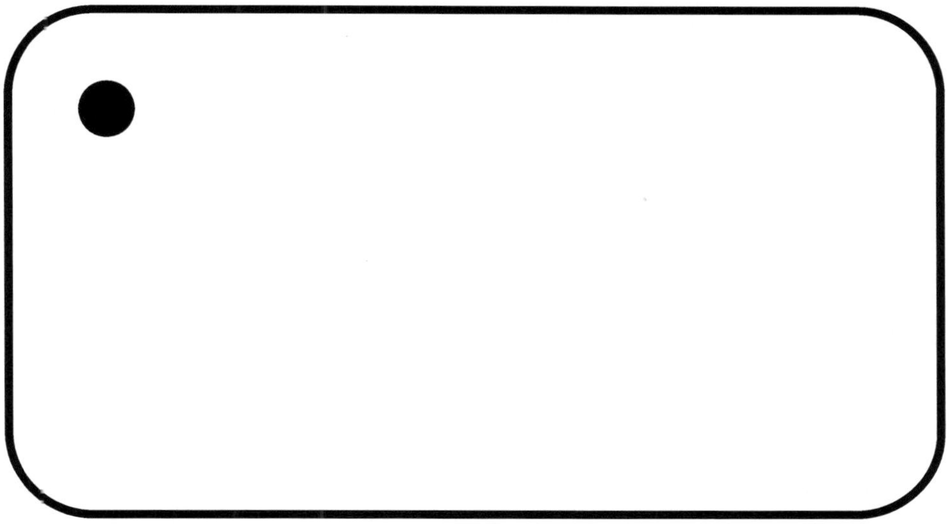

1. Print out this page onto white card.
2. Add your illustration and / or text.
3. Laminate on both sides.
4. Cut out the fans.
5. Make a hole on the black dot using a hole punch.
6. Link the cards together using a keyring circlet.

Coping Strategies

You might also find it useful to try out Situation or Prompt Cards, which function as a reminder or action prompt to help your son or daughter to manage situations in school, reducing anxiety and panic by providing them with a set of steps to follow. You may have identified some potential scenarios in the 'Let's talk about' activity earlier in this book.

First, discuss these scenarios with your child and school staff, focusing upon:

- How they can and should be managed
- Actions that your son or daughter needs to take
- Helpful responses from teachers or other school staff
- Responses or reactions that may create further difficulties

Actions or steps can then be written onto the Situation Cards. Situations might include:

- Getting lost
- Forgetting homework or PE kit
- Feeling unwell
- Feeling unsafe
- Lesson transitions
- What to do / where to go at lunch time
- What to do / where to go at break time
- Unexpectedly beginning a menstrual period
- Arriving late for school or for a lesson

Situation or Prompt Cards

1. Buy some blank or lined index cards.
2. Discuss and agree the steps to be taken with school staff.
3. Write out the steps as short, clear instructions.
4. Add an illustration if necessary.
5. Laminate on both sides.
6. Make a hole in the corner using a hole punch.
7. Link the cards together using a keyring circlet.

If I am feeling unwell and need to leave the class

1. Raise my hand to get the teacher's attention.
2. Wait for my teacher to respond to me.
3. Say:

   "I don't feel well, please may I leave the classroom".
4. Go to the bathroom first if I need to.
5. Go to Mrs White in room B4 on the second floor.

If I am lost and cannot find my way to class

1. Walk up to a student or a teacher and say:
2. "Excuse me. I can't find my classroom."
3. Listen to the instructions.
4. Say:

   "Thank you. Could you show me the way?"

Sorting out other difficulties

Whilst Situation Cards can be used in circumstances which might be predicted or anticipated, other scenarios require quite specific solutions. In Part 2 of this workbook, the section called 'Things That Can Help Me' introduces students to the **7 Steps Problem Sorter**. Students are encouraged to use this technique with a good friend, or an older brother or sister, or parents / carers / guardians. The seven steps to sorting problems are:

1. **Do not panic.** Think about:
2. **WHO** is creating the problem?
3. **WHY** is the problem, a problem?
4. **HOW** can the problem be solved?
5. **WHAT** might happen next if you followed your plan of action?
6. **WHEN and WHERE** could you activate your plan?
7. **CHOOSE** the best solution.

It's a good idea to practice managing this technique by modelling or demonstrating the steps using examples or social stories. Suggestions for practice activities are provided in Part Two of this workbook.

If you are concerned that your son or daughter is feeling stressed or anxious, and this is affecting their sleep, listening to some gentle music at bedtime is a good way of introducing a calm and relaxing atmosphere. Use a CD player or similar, and not a smart phone or tablet (too much temptation to play games). Soft water sounds or acoustic music are ideal. There are also many commercial **Biofeedback** stress devices on the market, which everyone in the family may find useful. They measure physiological changes in your body, such as your heart rate and skin temperature, using a sensor that you hold or attach to your fingers or hand. The sensors plug into your computer and use computer graphics to help you manage stress and anxiety by helping you to control breathing, relax your muscles, and think positive thoughts. For example, the initial screen image might portray a tree in winter, and as the sensor picks up changes in physiological responses, the tree gradually begins to bloom in front of your eyes. A good example of a reputable Biofeedback device is the **PIP** which has been clinically trialled https://thepip.com/en-eu/.

Managing the School Part of School

Helping your child to manage the school experience remotely is one of the hardest parts of being a parent. However, you will be less anxious and more confident as the years go on, if you resist the temptation to do everything on their behalf. Instead, begin this journey by doing things **together,** using prompts to build independence, and gradually phasing these out.

Talking to Teachers

A great deal of formal and informal information is given to students in school, and very little of this is written down. Sometimes, teachers are in a hurry to give instructions to students, perhaps at the beginning or end of the lesson, making it hard for young people to write everything down in their school journal or diary.

> Agreeing on methods of communication between home and school is vitally important, and is a task that you should address before the beginning of the school year.

Baseline communication of needs to relevant school staff should be agreed before school begins. You should also ask the Principal to remind staff at the beginning of term. Suggestions include:

- All teaching staff to be aware that a printed version of instructions / homework tasks needs to be provided to your student, or if the student is expected to write this down in the lesson, to **check** that this is accurate.
- Communication between parents and the learning support / Special Needs Assistant / class teacher is maintained using the home school diary, journal or by email.
- Regular progress meetings to be scheduled with learning support / Special Needs Assistant / class teacher, in addition to regular parent-teacher meetings.
- All teaching staff to be aware of the use of communication or prompt cards, or pre-agreed hand signals.
- All teaching staff to be aware of sensory processing difficulties.

It also helps to be mindful of the most appropriate / convenient times of the school day or week for contacting your student's teacher. Teaching staff have many other roles and responsibilities associated with the school, for example, organising and supervising clubs or activities, marking homework. It's a good idea to establish an agreed communication time at the beginning of the school year, and to stick to this.

How to Activate a Home / School Communication Arrangement

1. Agree on a strategy with the SENO, Special Needs Assistant, class teacher, learning support teacher i.e. a daily home / school journal, email, report card, notebook, or one page visual....

2. Make sure that this is formally written into the IEP or School Support Plan or Student Profile.

3. Talk to your child about their role in this communication strategy. In the beginning, this may only mean ensuring that the journal / card / communication page is taken out of their bag and handed to the teacher, and goes back in the bag and is

given to parents. This role can be extended later as part of developing self-advocacy.

4. Emphasise the importance of this exchange of information as a source of help and assistance for everyone. For example, it is advantageous for teachers to know if your child did not sleep or has had a change in medication, or if there has been an upsetting event at home.

5. Make it as easy as possible by restricting the amount of writing. Teachers do not have time to read a half page commentary at the beginning of the day. However, tick boxes, lists or bullet point messages are more likely to be read and responded to. Limit the exchange to critical information.

6. If the school uses a homework diary, journal, or notebook, make sure that there is space to record items to bring to and from school, and messages. If this is not the case, you can use a lined note book and lay the page out as follows:

Home School Log	
Date:	
Homework:	**Time spent on homework:**
1	
2	
3	
4	
Things to take home:	**Things to take to school:**
1	**1**
2	**2**
3	**3**
4	**4**
Message for school:	**Message for home:**

Photocopy the **Pack-A-Schoolbag Checklist** template on the next page. You can laminate this and keep it beside the timetable or place it inside a plastic sleeve and use a non-permanent marker. Or you could copy the checklist onto a small whiteboard which can be sourced from a stationery or office supply shop.

Pack-A-Schoolbag Checklist

What lessons do I have tomorrow? What are the names of the teachers? Which rooms are the lessons in? Where do I go at break time? Where do I go at lunchtime? What books do I need to put in my bag?

- ☐ English
- ☐ Maths
- ☐ Geography
- ☐ History
- ☐ Religion
- ☐ Language
- ☐ Homework
- ☐ School diary
- ☐ Pencil case
- ☐ Calculator
- ☐ Packed lunch
- ☐ PE clothes
- ☐ Science
- ☐ Money
- ☐ Forms

Using a Visual Timetable

> Your son or daughter may have used a visual timetable in primary school and it is essential to continue this support for managing schedules and belongings in secondary school.

- Enlist the help of your young person to make a wall timetable.
- Use an A2 sheet of paper or larger, or the blank side of a piece of wrapping paper, wallpaper, or poster.
- Photocopy the card templates to make your own symbol cards. Laminate and cut them out. You can stick them to the paper or whiteboard using double sided tape or poster putty so that they can be moved around.
- Alternatively, purchase a pack of blank playing cards from a craft shop, cut them in half, and draw and label your own symbols.
- Display the timetable in a family space such as the kitchen.
- You could also draw the timetable - use washable marker pens - on a whiteboard, or the inside of a cupboard door. I have also done this on the inside of a wardrobe door.
- With your student, model how to use the timetable to check lessons and activities for the following day.
- Remind your student of the name of the teacher for each lesson, and the location of the classroom. Check the route to the classroom.
- Make a list together of the items needed for the following day.
- Check whether additional items are required for special activities or events.
- Supervise your student in locating these things.
- Supervise them to pack these things in their bag, but do not do this for them.

Lunch	Break	School trip	Holiday

Art	Music	Drama	PE
Day off	Library	Computer	Homework
English	Geography	History	Science
Language	Physics	Chemistry	Biology
Maths	Business		

Managing school books and lockers

As students study more subjects at secondary school, there is a significant increase in the number of text books and workbooks that your child will need to transport on a daily basis together with additional items such as PE / sports clothes and equipment. For this reason, many secondary schools provide lockers in which students can keep most of their books and belongings. They may be given a key for the locker, or you might be given a code for a combination lock.

It's useful to check this out well in advance of the beginning of school, and have a few practice runs with lock combinations. Find out the procedure for getting a duplicate key if the original is lost. Go through this process with your son or daughter. This area of school can be quite noisy and very crowded as everyone is trying to sort out their books and bags. It can be a bit of a trouble spot for teasing or other 'high jinks'. It might help if your child used their locker at a quiet time, perhaps at break or lunchtime. If your child experiences difficulties with sensory processing, discuss this with the school before the beginning of the year, and arrange for them to have a locker in a suitable place. For example:

- at the end of a row
- a top or bottom locker which better suits their height
- in a quieter space
- in a place that is close to the staff room

It can be very difficult to keep on top of taking the right books to and from school. You can get around this problem by keeping a second set of books at home. This can really help with relieving some of the stress, and is a good solution to the problem of forgetting to bring books home. These need not be expensive if you buy a set of second hand copies. Alternatively, you can purchase eBook / digital versions directly from the publisher, that can be stored on an iPad or eReader. Discuss the possibility of using portable digital versions with the school.

Helping with Homework

It is very likely that your son or daughter will receive homework every night, and often this may entail work for more than one subject. Whilst the workload may be quite manageable to begin with, it will increase over time. Teachers do not consult with each other about homework assignments, or when these will be allocated, so on some days there may be a significant amount of homework, and on other days very little. The following techniques or strategies will help; item numbers 10 and 11 are very important. If homework is too difficult or the amount is overwhelming, this needs to be raised with the teacher. Doing your child's homework for them raises false expectations and causes problems later.

Acting as a scribe for your child is very tempting if it means homework can be done more quickly, especially if your son or daughter finds it difficult to put their thoughts into writing. Although this might seem to be a long way into the future, this can cause significant problems for managing college or employment. If handwriting formation or speed, or 'getting things down on paper' is causing difficulty, a technological solution is preferable. This might mean agreeing with the teacher that homework can be completed on an iPad or laptop, if necessary using voice recognition speech-to-text software, for example, **Dragon Naturally Speaking**. Structured touch typing programmes are available that simultaneously improve reading and spelling, such as **Touch Type Read and Spell.**

If your son or daughter has difficulty with reading accuracy and / or speed, investigate digital textbooks – almost all publishers provide these. Adobe PDF documents and eBooks have built in 'read aloud' functions that can assist with reading comprehension. If necessary, agree with the school that using a tablet which stores all of the electronic textbooks, is required.

1. Help to plan out extended pieces of coursework or projects over a period of days or weeks;
2. Check the homework diary together each day;
3. Encourage a set time slot for homework;
4. Check the minimum and maximum time requirement for homework e.g. 45 minutes per evening;
5. Identify a calm, quiet, clean, and tidy space to do homework;
6. Make sure your child is neither too cold or too warm, neither hungry nor thirsty;
7. Make sure that mobile phones, tablets, and computers are switched off;
8. Help with homework but do not take over;
9. Keep an eye on the time spent on homework. Check that they do not spend too much or too little time on each piece;
10. Try not to act as a scribe for your child; invest early in technology.
11. Don't do the work for them;
12. Confirm to the school that homework was supervised for the required amount of time e.g. "John did not manage to complete all of the set homework, he did spend the recommended 45 minutes of study time on this task."

Your child should not be spending more than the recommended amount of time on homework. If it is taking longer than expected, you need to discuss a modified homework load with the school.

Participating in School Life

An important part of managing the early weeks of transition, is to ensure that your son or daughter recognises that they are part of a wider community. Social acceptance is very important, and activities and strategies are provided in Part Two of this workbook, focusing on making friends and talking to people. Helping your young person to be aware of their role and place within the school community, is very important.

Reputation and achievement

Not all students like, enjoy or are interested in the same extra-curricular activities, sports, clubs, or events. However, it is important for them to be aware of any specific achievements for which the school is known: have they been super successful in a particular sport, for example, football, swimming, rugby. Do they have an award-winning debating team, or a reputation for producing young scientists? Even if your son or daughter does not want to participate in these aspects of school life, they should be aware of their importance within the school, and the importance of being a spectator and / or a supporter. Build this into the 'Getting to Know My New School' activities.

After school socialising

Hanging out with friends after school and at the weekend is a very important part of adolescence, but can be fraught with anxieties for some young people. One way of building conversational and social skills, which can increase social invitations, is to encourage participation with peers in group activities such as clubs, scouting, or sports. Explore these opportunities both within and outside of school. Practicing specific conversational scripts builds confidence, for example, how to introduce yourself, what to do when you enter a room for the first meeting of a group.

Managing social media

Using the Internet and social media can provide significant benefits to young people who find it difficult to socialise: it is easier to talk to people and 'be yourself', it is a means to making new friends, it is easier to find other young people who share specific interests, it is a way of participating in group social activities. Some schools use Facebook and Instagram accounts to communicate news about events, clubs, sporting achievements etc., and the use of WhatsApp groups to share ideas and work on projects, is becoming widespread. This overlap in use between arranging school and personal social events, meet ups and hangouts, means that sometimes safety and rules for using social media, can become blurred.

Fortunately, there are many resources available to parents for monitoring use of social media and the Internet. Materials written specifically for young people include **Share Aware lessons from the NSPCC**. Check government guidelines and agencies, for example, the following social media guidance for parents is offered by the UK Council for Child Internet Safety and is public sector information licensed under the Open Government Licence v3.0.

Online Safety

Social networking is hugely popular. Many young people are sophisticated in the way they use social media apps and websites, tailoring their communication for different audiences, and accessing them from a range of devices including smartphones, tablets, and games consoles.

But social media, like all forms of public communication, comes with some risks. Not all of these risks turn into actual problems; and if children never face any risks, they never learn how to deal with them. By helping your child understand what the risks are, you can play a big part in preventing them from turning into problems.

1. Understand the risks children may need to deal with:

What they might see or do:

- Seeing or sharing of violent, sexual and pornographic content
- Inaccurate or false information and extreme views
- Promotion of harmful behaviours including self-harm, anorexia and suicide
- Over-sharing of personal information
- Actively or unintentionally getting involved in bullying or hurtful behaviour

Who they might meet:

- People who might bully, intimidate or frighten
- People posing behind fake profiles for:
    - Mischief-making
    - Sexual grooming and stalking
    - Blackmail and extortion
    - Identity theft and hacking

How this could affect them:

- Fear of missing out leading to excessive Internet use
- Getting upset by things they have seen and being uncertain about what to do
- Engaging, or being pressured into engaging in more risky behaviour either by accident or by design
- Developing unrealistic, and perhaps depressing ideals of body image and gender
- Becoming subject to peer pressure or interactions that are intense or too difficult to handle
- Creating an online reputation that may create problems for them in the future

2. Practical tips to help minimise the risks your child might face

It's good practice for apps and websites to have safety advice and well-designed safety features which can make a real difference to how safe your child will be when using them. Work through safety and privacy features on the apps that your child is using, or might use. Make sure they understand the point of these and how to use them. Don't be put off by believing your child knows more than you: the tools are actually quite easy to manage.

- Ask them to show you which social media apps they use and what they like about them. Talk about how they use them and what makes them so engaging
- Explain how you can use privacy settings to make sure only approved friends can see posts & images
- Check if any of their apps have 'geo-location' enabled, sharing their location unintentionally
- Show them how to report offensive comments or block people who upset them
- Check 'tagging' settings so that when others are posting or sharing photos online, your child's identity is not revealed. Also, get people's consent before sharing photos
- Encourage your child to come and talk to you if they see anything that upsets them

3. Keep talking and stay involved

In a mobile age, children can't be completely protected, even by the best privacy controls; another child may use different settings. So it's important to keep talking to your child about the implications of social media. Getting a sense of what they think is a useful place to start; you may be surprised by how much thought they may have given to the issues.

Encourage your child to think carefully about the way they, and others behave online, and how they might deal with difficult situations.

- People may not always be who they say they are online: how can this create problems?
- Why is it unwise to meet anyone in the real world that you've only ever met online?
- Even if you think your messages are private, remember that words and images can always be captured and broadcast.
- People present themselves differently online - do they really look like that? Are they always having that good a time?
- Be aware that screens, and especially being anonymous, can lead people to say things they wouldn't say to someone's face.
- What does being a good friend and a likeable person online look like?
- There can be pressure to be part of a particular group online or to be seen to be following a certain set of ideas
- How can you take a step back and make your own decisions?

4. More information

- www.internetmatters.org
- www.nspcc.org.uk/onlinesafety
- www.parentzone.org.uk
- http://allaboard2017.ie/online-resources/
- https://www.webwise.ie/

Tips for school trips

School trips teach students about the world outside of the classroom. Imaginative and well organised visits can be engaging and rewarding experiences, but they may also cause anticipatory anxiety and distress for some young people. Most difficulties arise because of insufficient information or misunderstandings, so preparation is key.

- ☐ **Ask about planned school trips** at the beginning of the school year, and thereafter on a regular basis: "Are there any school visits coming up this month?" Check with your student's SNA.
- ☐ **Plan in advance.** Highlight the trip on a wall calendar and have a 'count down' conversation once or twice a week. Increase this to once a day as the trip draws nearer.
- ☐ Make sure that your student knows that the day before and the day after the school trip, will roll out as usual.
- ☐ Talk about the **what, why, when, where, who, and how**, e.g.: **where** are they going (history museum), **why** (studying ancient Rome), **when** (31st March from 10.00 a.m. to 4.00 p.m.), **where** (name of town or city), **who** (which teachers and any other adults that your student may not be familiar with), **how** (by coach leaving from school park and returning to school car park, taking 1.5 hours for each journey).
- ☐ **Research the venue online with your student**. Check the website for maps, floor plans, images of the buildings and outside spaces.
- ☐ **Talk about any sensory issues** that might arise from researching the venue. Talk about the possibility of being too hot or cold, noise and crowds. Practice a script for communicating this to the teacher, and how to ask for a break or to leave the venue.
- ☐ **Ask for the planned schedule** in terms of how time will be spent (e.g. first we are going to visit the ground floor exhibition…) and breaks.
- ☐ **Talk to your young person about their seating preference** on the bus (front seat, back seat, left side, right side). Who will they sit with, an SNA or a teacher, or do they have a classmate that they need to be near? Communicate this to the teacher.
- ☐ **Ask the teacher(s) to use a verbal prompt before each transition**, either to the entire party, or individually e.g. "in five minutes, we will be arriving at the museum, and then we will exit the bus, and wait in a group outside the entrance." Make sure that they know to alert your student if they wear ear defenders.
- ☐ **Find out which adults will be going on the trip**. Explain who these people are – use images if possible - what they do, and why they are on the trip.
- ☐ Explain why it is important for your young person to do exactly what they are told by a supervising teacher.
- ☐ **Have a plan in place for managing meltdowns**. Discuss this with the teacher in charge and SNA.
- ☐ **Make sure that teaching staff are aware of medication**, and have details of dosage and timing.
- ☐ **Packed lunch or café / restaurant?** If necessary, ensure that the teachers know that your student will be bringing their own lunch. Make sure they have plenty of water.

Individual Transition Plans

Individual Transition Plan

1. Personal Information
2. Background
3. Diagnostic Information
4. Transition Assessment
    - ☒ Strengths
    - ☒ Academic Challenges
    - ☒ Environmental Challenges
    - ☒ Recommendations for Management of Academic Requirements
    - ☒ Recommendations for Management of the School Environment
    - ☒ Recommendations for Differentiated and Inclusive Teaching
    - ☒ Recommendations for Special Needs Assistant

Prepared by:

If your child has special educational needs or a disability, he or she may need a transition plan to support the move to secondary school. You should discuss this well before the end of primary or elementary school, with current and prospective teachers and any other professional involved in you child's care, such as psychologists or health professionals.

An Individual Transition Plan ensures that strengths, challenges, and needs, are communicated to school staff prior to the moment of transition. Some young people may have an Individual Education Plan, which also sets out these requirements.

Where this is not available or does not exist, an Individual Transition Plan fulfills the same function. It is completed by the primary school, in consultation with parents, the student, and support professionals, and captures information about:

- Special Educational Needs / Disabilities
- Support provided in primary school
- External professional supports
- Strengths and challenges
- Differentiated teaching requirements
- Physical and curriculum access requirements

You should request a transition planning meeting with the school principal, class teacher, special needs staff, and any other professionals who have been involved with your child.

Part 2: Getting to Know My New School

Moving to another school can be a tricky time, but it can also be exciting and fun! You can start this workbook at the end of primary or elementary school.

Finding Out

What does my new school look like?

Who will I meet?

What will I do?

Where will I go?

Talking About Changes

What is the same and what is different?

How does school work?

What will I learn?

Getting Organised

Organising myself and the things I need for school

Travelling to and from school

Things That Can Help Me

Taking care of myself

Safe spaces

Making friends and getting along with people

Solving tricky situations

Finding Out

There are a lot of things to find out about your new school. If you collect it all in this workbook, you will be able to read over it as many times as you like before you start at your new school. You may not be able to find out all of this information immediately, but you can ask someone at home to help you.

My school is called:

____

____

Address:

____

____

Telephone number: ______________________________

E-mail: ______________________________________

Website: _____________________________________

School crest or badge:

School Visit

Before the end of your last year in primary or elementary school you will visit your new secondary school or high school, either with your class or with your parents. Maybe both. You may have an opportunity to go on more than one visit. Think about some of the questions that you would like to ask. These might be about:

- ✓ Lunch and break times
- ✓ Clothes
- ✓ Lessons and subjects
- ✓ School rules
- ✓ Homework
- ✓ Sports and PE
- ✓ People in school

Write down some of the questions that you would like to ask about your new school.

1. ____

2. ____

3. ____

4. ____

5. ____

6. ____

7. ____

8. ____

9. ____

After your school visit, it's a good idea to talk about it with your parents or your class teacher.

What did you like about the school?

What didn't you like about the school?

Who did you meet?

How was it different from your primary school?

Is there anything you are still not sure about? There are probably a lot of things you still want to know. In the next few pages we are going to find out more about your new school.

What does my new school look like?

You can visit your secondary school and take photographs. Or you can search for photographs and maps on the Internet.

The outside of my new school

Aerial photograph

Sports area

Lunch room or cafeteria

School uniform

Find a picture of your new school uniform. You can look in the school brochure or print one out from the school website.

Find a picture of your sports or PE kit. You can look in the school brochure or print one out from the school website.

Who will I meet?

In primary school the teacher stays with the class for the whole day. In secondary school, there is a teacher who is responsible for organising your class or 'form', but you may only see them first thing in the morning. They usually teach a subject such as History or Maths. For the rest of the day you will go to a different classroom for each subject, and you will probably have a different teacher for each subject.

In some secondary schools where there are a lot of students, there may be more than one class group for each year, so there will also be a teacher who is in charge of each year group. In some schools, if a student does not feel well they go to the school office, and the receptionist, secretary or administrator will call their parents. In some larger schools, there may be a school nurse and a 'sick room', infirmary, or First Aid room where students can go and lie down until their parents come to fetch them. Find out more about these people and what they do in your school:

The name of the Principal or Headteacher is:

What do they do?

When will I see them?

The name of the school secretary or office person is:

What do they do?

When will I see them?

The name of the resource or learning support teacher is:

What do they do?

When will I see them?

Can you find the names of other teachers? They might be on the school website:

- English teacher
- Maths
- Art
- Science
- History
- Geography
- PE
- Home economics
- Languages
- Resource / Learning support

There are other people in school that you can go to if you are feeling unwell or anxious, or are not sure what to do. Sometimes this might be a School Nurse, or the Guidance Counsellor, or someone in the school office.

Go-to people that I can ask for help:

How many students are there in your new school?

How many people will there be in your class?

What will I do?

What subjects will you learn in your new school?

1.

2.

3.

4.

5.

6.

7.

8.

What sports are there in your new school?

What other activities can you do?

Where will I go?

It can be difficult to find your way around a new environment. Before you visit your new school, your parents could ask for a copy of the floor plan. Or, you could ask your class teacher or SNA to help you make your own floor plan when you visit the school. You could photocopy this and highlight or colour the rooms that you will be using in your first year. If you visit the school with your parents, you could make a video of the different routes and classrooms on a mobile phone or tablet.

Your new school might hold events like a Christmas Fair or a concert or a bake sale. Ask someone at home to let you know when this happens so that you can visit your new school and take a look around.

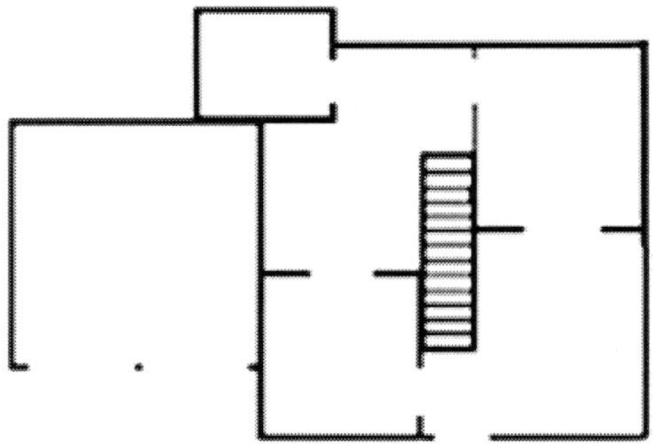

Find out where the following spaces are in your new school:

- Your class home room.
- The school dining room or cafeteria.
- The school library.
- Quiet areas.
- School gym and changing rooms.
- The toilet areas.
- The School Principal or Head Teacher's office.
- The secretary's office.
- The sick room / school nurse.
- The main student entrance.
- The staff room.

Getting Organised and Managing Time

In this section, we are going to think about organising yourself and your belongings.

Ready and on Time

Your new school might be further away from where you live than your primary school, so it might take longer to get there, and therefore you may need to leave the house earlier than you have been used to. How long will it take you to do the following things in the morning? Time yourself and write the number of minutes in the box.

☐ Have a wash / shower.

☐ Get dressed and clean your teeth.

☐ Eat your breakfast.

☐ Check your timetable.

☐ Check that you have the right books and your homework in your bag.

☐ Check that you have packed your lunch / lunch money.

Organising Things for School

You will have a LOT of school books to carry so it is important that your bag is the right size and is comfortable on your back. Find a picture of a school bag that you would like. Where can you buy this bag from? How much does it cost? You will need different clothing to change into for PE. What do you need to put in your PE bag?

The night before you should:

- ☐ Check your timetable to see what lessons you have the following day.
- ☐ Check your homework diary or school journal to see if there are special things that you need to bring.
- ☐ Check that you have done all your homework.
- ☐ Make a list of everything you need to take to school.

Before leaving the house to go to school, you must make sure that you have everything you need for that day. The best time to do this is the night before, so that you do not run out of time, or become anxious or stressed. Some days you will need extra equipment. This will depend on the lessons you have that day. For example, you might need to take a form or money. Ask someone to photocopy this page for you to use. You need to look at your timetable and write down the things that you need for each day.

Day of the week	**Things I need to take to school**
Monday	
Tuesday	
Wednesday	
Thursday	
Friday	

Using a Locker in School

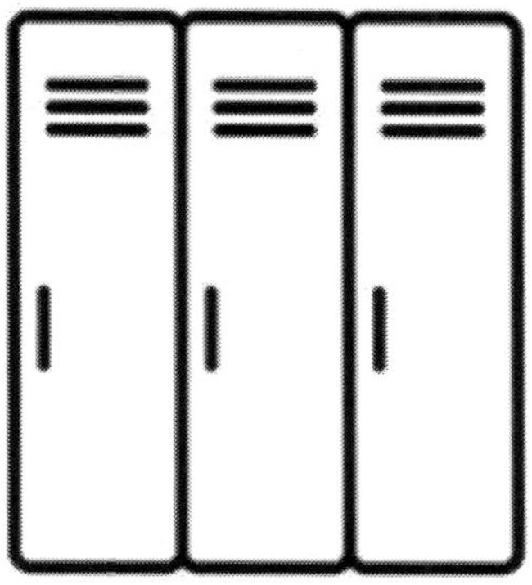

In secondary school, you will be studying more subjects than in primary school, and you will probably have too many books to take to school every day. Many secondary schools provide lockers in which students can keep most of their books, so that you do not have to take them all home every afternoon. You might be given a key for the locker, or you might be given a code for a combination lock.

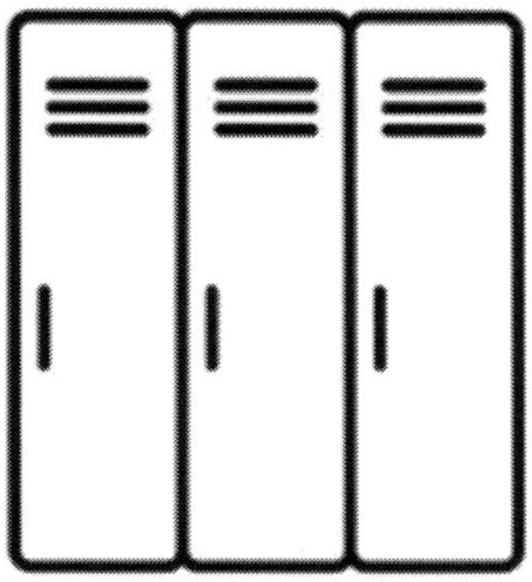

This area of school can be quite noisy and very crowded as everyone is trying to sort out their books and bags. It might help if you used your locker at a quiet time, perhaps at break or lunchtime. It can be very difficult to remember to take the right books to and from school, and sometimes the locker area can be very stressful. You can get around this problem by keeping a second set of books at home. School lockers are for school books and equipment. It is not a good idea to leave valuable things in your locker like jewellery or mobile phones.

Find out who you need to talk to if you lose your locker key.

Getting to and from School

If your new school is further away from your primary school you might need to get there by car, bus, or train. You might be able to walk or cycle. It's a good idea to know about different ways to go to and from school. Ask someone at home to help you with some of these questions. You may need to practice your journey and look for some of the information on the Internet.

You could write out a list of directions on a card and keep it in your bag.

If you are going to walk 	
Who will you walk with?	
How long will the journey take?	
What time do you have to leave?	
Do you know how to get there?	
Do you know how to get back?	
Do you need to practice?	

If you are going to cycle 	
Who will you cycle with?	
How long will the journey take?	
What time do you have to leave?	
Do you know how to get there?	
Where will you leave your bike in school?	
Do you need a lock?	

If you are going to go by car 	
Who will drive you?	
How long will the journey take?	
What time do you have to leave?	
What time will you be collected?	
Where should you wait?	

If you are going by train / tram	
How long will the journey take?	
Who will go with you?	
What number / destination train / tram can you take?	
Where do you take it from?	
What time do you have to leave?	
How much does it cost?	
Where do you wait to take the train / tram home?	

If you are going to go by bus	
How long will the journey take?	
Who will go with you?	
What number / destination bus can you take?	
Is there a bus stop near your house?	
What time do you have to leave?	
How much does it cost?	
Is there a bus stop near to your school?	

Talking About Changes

When you start attending your new school, you will notice a difference in the way that students behave, the way in which school is organised, and how you spend your time. It's a good idea to think about these things before you move to another school and to talk to people at home about this.

Same or different?

Let's think about some of the things that could be different about your new school. Some young people worry about these changes, so it's good to talk about this with your parents, or carer, or an older brother or sister, or other relatives. Some people feel anxious about:

- ☑ Wearing different clothes
- ☑ Making friends
- ☑ Meeting new teachers
- ☑ Sports and PE
- ☑ Noises and smells
- ☑ Moving between places
- ☑ Lessons, subjects, and homework

We are going to think about how you feel about things that may be the same or different, and to help you, we are going to use a happiness scale:

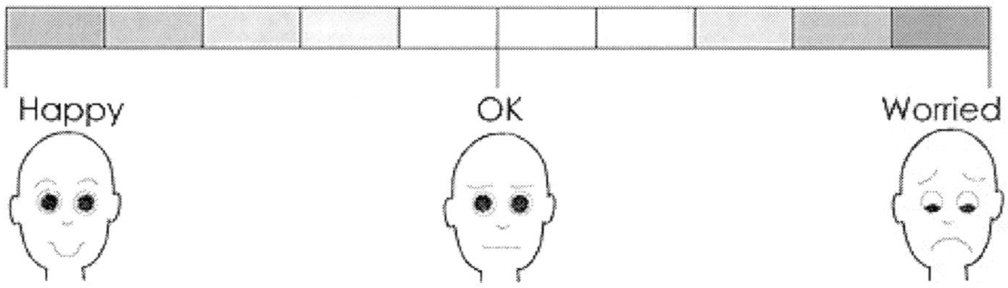

Clothes

The clothes that you wear in primary school may be quite different to the uniform in your new school. In primary school, children may be allowed to wear more casual clothing such as a tracksuit or a hoody. In some secondary schools, you will almost certainly have to wear a tie if you are a boy, or a skirt if you are a girl, but sometimes not. You found out about your new uniform earlier in this book. How do you feel about wearing these clothes? Do you find that some clothes are too scratchy or flappy? Have you tried on the different parts of this uniform (skirt, trousers, shirt, jumper) in a shop?

Is there anything that worries you or makes you feel anxious about wearing your new uniform? Mark a place on the line which describes how you feel about this.

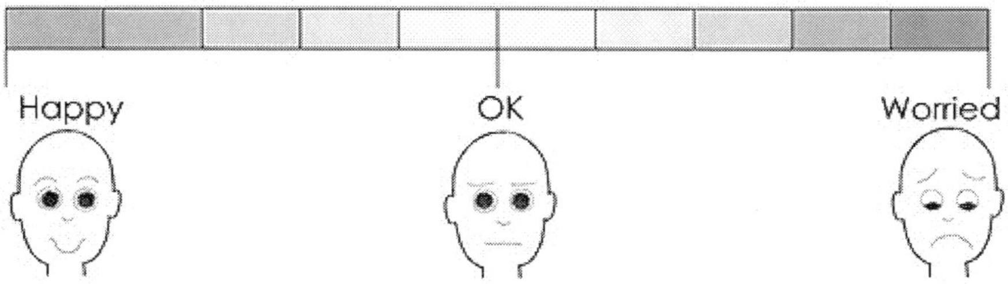

What might help you to feel less worried about wearing the uniform?

Friends

Not all young people move to the same secondary school. Sometimes it will depend upon where they live, and if there are enough places for them in the school. This could mean that only one or two people from your primary school will be moving with you to your new school. It's good to make new friends, but it can also be a little bit scary going to a new place if you don't know anyone else. Find out if friends and other people in your primary school are going to your secondary school. How are you feeling about meeting new people and making new friends in your next school?

Is there anything that worries you or makes you feel anxious about meeting new people, and making new friends? Mark a place on the line which describe how you feel about meeting new people.

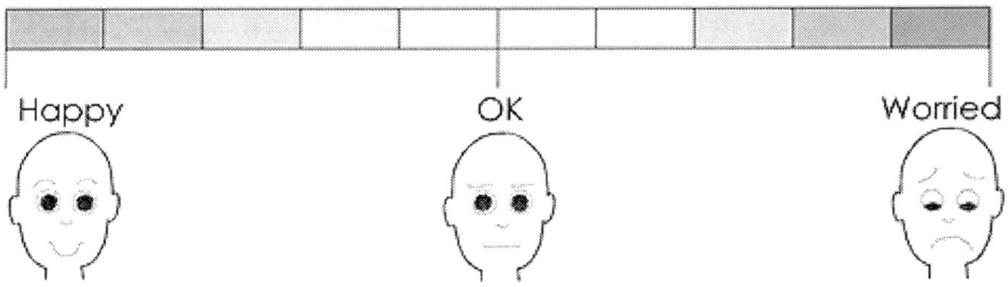

What would help you to feel less worried about making new friends?

Teachers

One of the main differences between primary and secondary school is that there are more teachers. In some schools one teacher might teach two subjects so, for example, you might have the same teacher for both German and PE. Your class teacher is responsible for looking after everyone in your class, and you may see them in your 'home' classroom each morning. Your class teacher is the person you should go to if you have any problems. How are you feeling about working with more teachers in your next school?

Is there anything that worries you or makes you feel anxious about having new teachers? Mark a place on the line which describes how you feel about this.

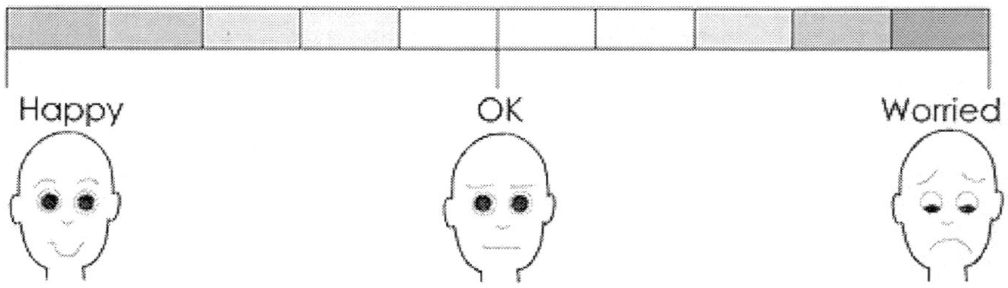

What might help you to feel less worried about working with so many new teachers?

Sports and PE

You may not have had to change your clothes for PE or Games lessons in primary school. In secondary school, you will usually have to change into a different set of clothes, sometimes called a 'PE kit'. You will probably change your clothes in an area near to the sports hall, sometimes called 'the changing rooms'. You might also be told to have a shower after the PE lesson. There may also be a wider variety of sporting activities such as football, rugby, tennis, badminton, cross-country running, basketball, or hockey. Although you may not like some or all of the sports and games activities in your new school, it's important to know about the sports teams in your school and whether they have won any competitions.

Is there anything that worries you or makes you feel anxious about PE lessons or sports activities? Mark a place on the line which describes how you feel about this.

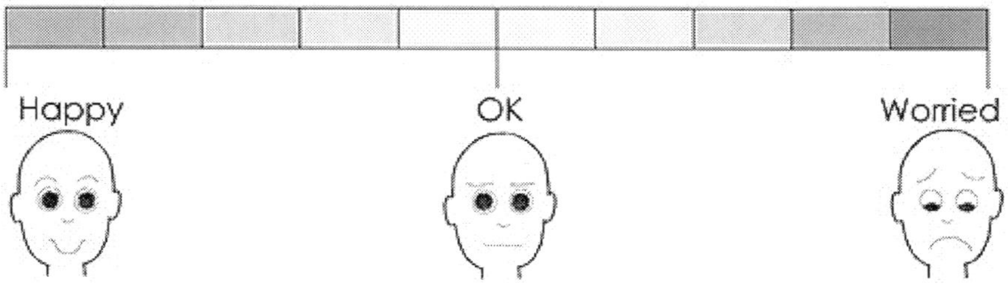

What might help you to feel less worried about PE or sports activities?

Noise and smells

Your new secondary school will be a much bigger place than primary school. There will be more and probably taller buildings, and larger outside spaces. This means that there will be more young people and adults around you. So, there may be more noise in general from people talking as they move from classroom to classroom. It may be especially noisy in the dining hall or lunch room. Toilets can also be noisy places as the tiles on the wall make sounds echo, and there can be a lot of background noise from hand drying machines. The fire alarm may be different to the one used in your primary school. Because the school is so much bigger, in some secondary schools, announcements are made over a loud speaker, and a bell might ring at the end of every lesson.

Is there anything that worries you or makes you feel anxious about noises or smells in your new school? Mark a place on the line which describes how you feel.

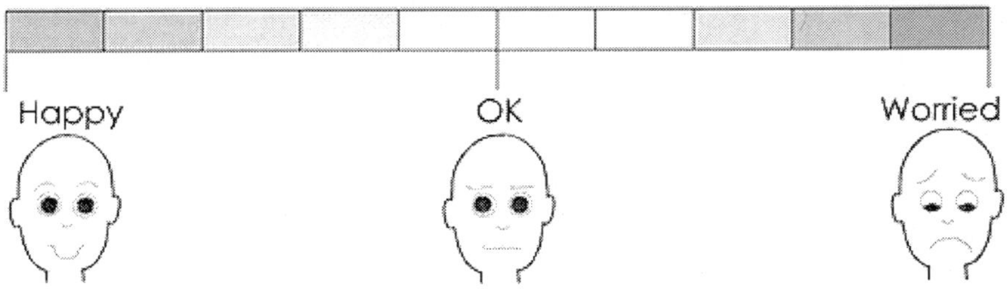

What might help you to feel less worried about noises and smells in your new school?

Lunchtime and breaks

In your primary school, you might have eaten a hot meal or brought a packed lunch to eat in the dining room, the assembly hall, or your classroom. This space will probably be similar in your secondary school, but much bigger. There will certainly be more students so it will be noisier. Break times will also be quite different. You won't see small children running around, but there will be groups of students talking together. Some of them will be much older and taller than you.

Is there anything that worries you or makes you feel anxious about lunchtime or break times? Mark a place on the line which describes how you feel about this.

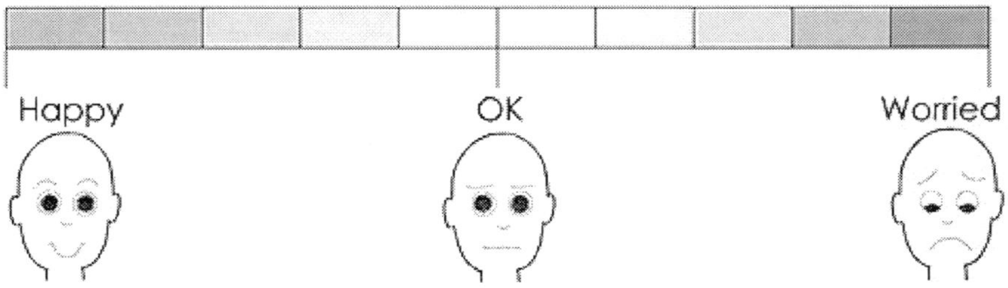

What might help you to feel less worried about managing lunchtime and break times?

Lessons, subjects, and homework

The school day is longer in secondary school as you will usually have six hours of lessons as well as lunch and break times. The school day is divided into lessons which last for about 45 minutes, with one subject studied in each lesson. Sometimes two lessons are tied together in a 'double lesson' or 'double period'. In primary school, you probably stayed in your classroom and your teacher helped you with reading, spelling, and writing, and taught you other things such as Art and Craft, or PE. In secondary school, there is a teacher for each subject, and most of the time you move to a different classroom for each lesson. You will study at least seven subjects, and your school might decide to have extra short courses. You will be given homework to do every day after school.

Is there anything that worries you or makes you feel anxious about having more subjects to study or more homework to do in the evening? Mark a place on the line which describes how you feel about this.

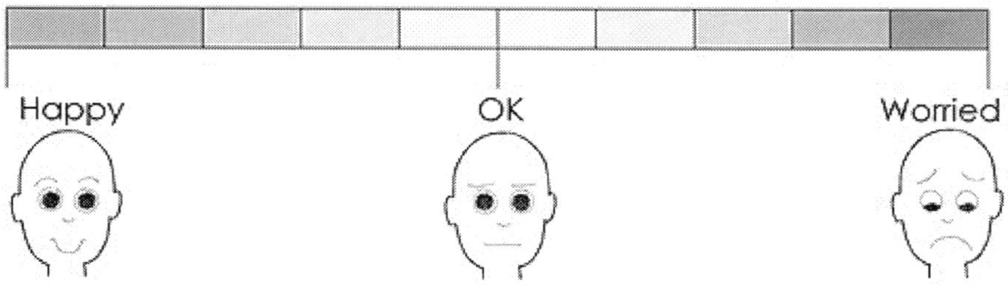

What might help you to feel less worried about managing more subjects and homework?

School Routines

We are going to find out more about how your school day is organised. The length of the school day will probably be slightly longer, as you will have more subjects and more lessons. What time does school begin and end? You can mark this on the clock faces below. Does school finish at the same time every day? Which days are different?

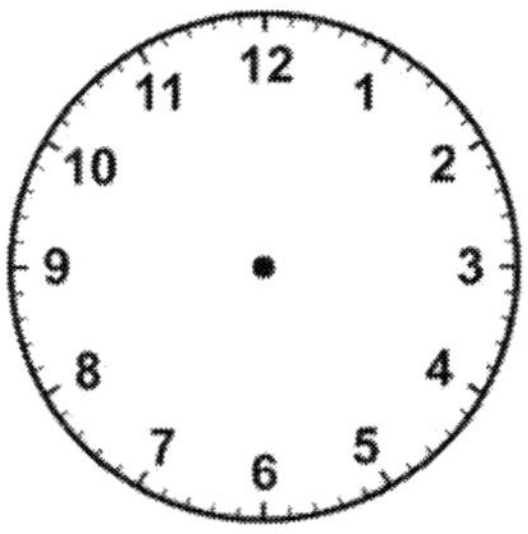

School begins at

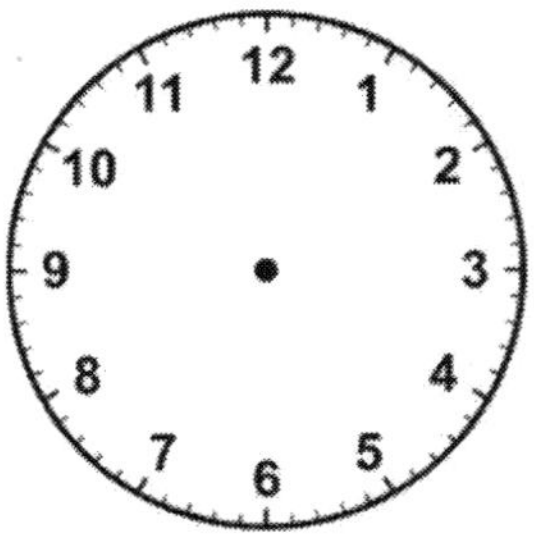

School ends at

_ _ : _ _   _ _ : _ _

Are there activities that happen on the same day every week, for example, a school assembly?

Lessons usually last for 50 minutes, and in some schools even one hour. This is to allow students time to move from one classroom to another, or to fetch books and other equipment from their lockers. Some subjects might have two lessons running together and this called a 'double' lesson or sometimes a 'double period'. Colour in a block of time on the clock to represent a single and a double lesson.

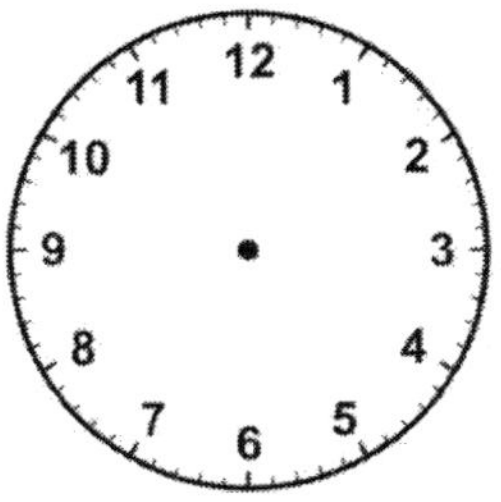

A single lesson

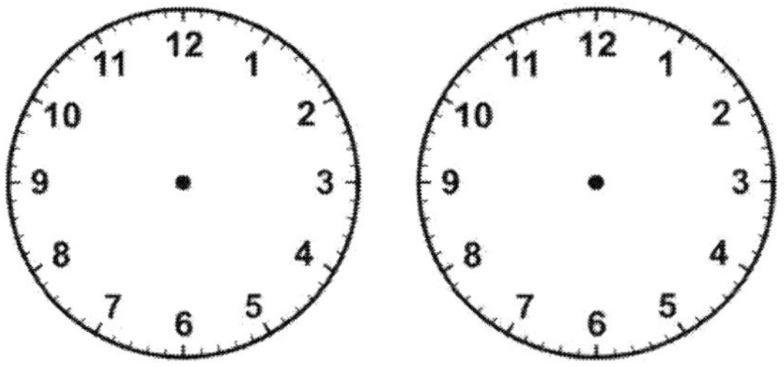

A double lesson

In most schools, a bell will ring when the lesson has finished. The teacher will tell everyone to close their books and move on to the next lesson. Sometimes, the teacher will tell you quickly about:

- ✓ The homework that they want you to do.
- ✓ What you will be doing the next time they see you.
- ✓ Things they may want you to bring in to school.
- ✓ Trips or activities that may be happening in the future.

You must pack up your books, pens, and any other things you have on the desk, and put them into your bag. You will need to leave the classroom and travel to a different classroom for the next lesson. If people in your class are going to the same lesson, you can follow them. What do you need to do at the end of the lesson?

1. Put pencils, pens, ruler etc. back in your pencil case.
2. Put your books and pencil case back into your school bag.
3. Check your timetable to see what lesson you have next.
4. If you are unsure, ask someone.

Do you know anyone who is in secondary school now? Ask them to show you their timetable.

Do not panic or worry if you don't hear or understand something that the teacher has said. You can:

- Say to someone sitting next to you "I didn't hear that, what did she say?"
- Put up your hand and ask the teacher to repeat the instructions.
- If you have a Special Needs Assistant or Classroom Assistant working with you, ask them to repeat the instructions so that you can write them down in your school journal or diary.

What happens in morning break?

About half way through the morning there will be a short break in lessons. You have a break time in your primary school, and this is when everyone goes out into the playground. Usually, everyone is running around, or playing a game. It can be quite noisy. Break time in secondary school is similar but there are many more people, and they are older and bigger than students in primary school. There is less running around but some people may play football or basketball. Find out when break time starts and finishes. Do you know anyone in secondary school? Ask them what they do at break times.

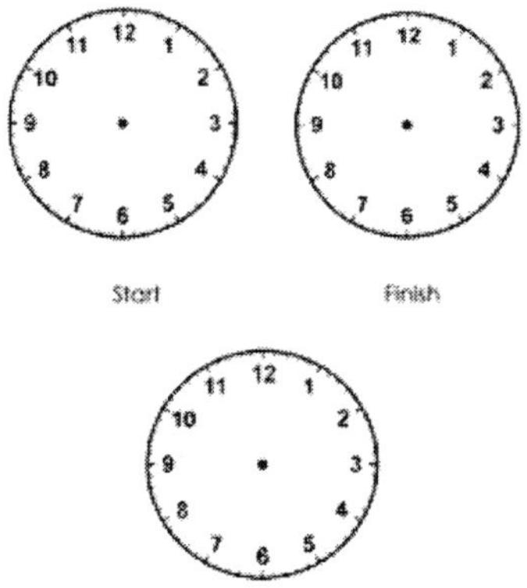

How long does break time last? Colour in a block of time on the clock to represent break time. You may be allowed to stay inside for break time, but you might have to go to a particular place or space, and not to a classroom.

Place	What you are allowed to do

What happens at lunchtime?

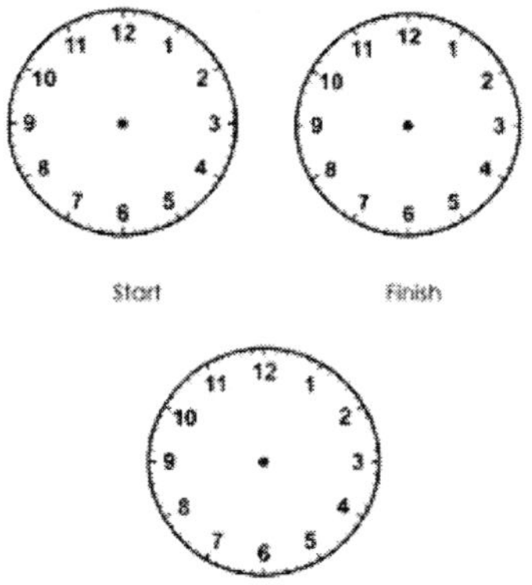

The lunch break is between morning and afternoon lessons. It is a time when you can mix with your friends, go to a lunchtime activity, and eat your lunch. How long does it last? Colour in a block of time on the clock to represent lunchtime.

Where do students have lunch?	
Is there hot food?	
How much does it cost?	
Is there a menu?	
Can you buy drinks and snacks?	

Some schools provide hot meals for students. Find out if your school does this and if they have a canteen, cafeteria, or dining room.

There may be different activities available in your new school during the lunch break. For example, you might be able to take part in sports or an activity club for board games, or Drama, or practice a musical instrument.

Lunchtime activities at my new school:

If you do not want to join in with an activity, and you do not want to go outside into the school grounds, you should find out where you can go and what you can do there. It's also handy to think about what you could do during break and lunchtime if you are on your own.

- Would you take a book to read whilst eating your lunch, or perhaps you like drawing?
- Would you be allowed to wear headphones and listen to music?
- Are you allowed to take electronic games?
- Is it possible to go to the library?

If you see someone else eating lunch on their own, you could say: "Is anyone else sitting here?" and sit down beside them.

Place	**What you are allowed to do**

Rules and Behaviour

There are a lot of rules in secondary school, and they are different to the rules in your primary school. Some of these are related to:

- How you talk to your teachers
- What you can and can't do during break and lunchtime
- Completing and handing in homework
- Arriving late to school

Because there will be many more students in your new secondary school, the school rules are likely to be different from those in your primary school. Think about how things might be different, how you will be expected to behave, and the reasons for this. Some schools have rules about moving between classes, for example, 'students must only walk on the right-hand side of the corridor'. Some schools have rules about wearing jewellery, length of hair, or bringing mobile phones to school. See if you can find the school rules on your new school website. Are these rules different from the ones in your primary school?

1. ______________________________

2. ______________________________

3. ______________________________

4. ______________________________

5. ______________________________

6. ______________________________

There are probably also rules about what to do if you are late coming in to school, and leaving the school premises during the day.

Are there any rules in particular that you think you need to talk about with someone?

Sorting Out Mistakes

If you do make a mistake or break a school rule, you should apologize and give a reason. If you accidentally upset another student or annoy a teacher, you should apologise immediately and explain what happened.

You need to make sure that you look as if you are sorry, and that you don't look cross, or as if you think it is a joke.

You can practice the conversation you might have with someone at home, for example, think about the following situations:

1. Knocking someone's schoolbag off their desk.
2. Forgetting your homework.
3. Spilling someone's drink in the lunchroom.
4. Bringing the wrong book to your lesson.

When you upset someone

If you accidentally bump into another student and make them drop something, apologize, and give a reason:

"I'm really sorry, are you OK? I didn't see you there."

When you forget something

If you forget a school book, your homework, your PE kit, or a form from your parents, do not worry. Everyone forgets things – even adults. Apologize and give a reason:

"I'm really sorry [teacher's name e.g. Mr Brown] but I forgot to put the (book, PE kit, homework, form) into my bag."

You can also use the **7 Steps Problem Sorter** on page 77.

Taking Care of Myself

In this part of the book we are going to think about the things you need to do to take care of yourself, which include personal care and hygiene, making friends, and managing tricky situations.

People need very specific things to be healthy and happy, such as:

Achieving goals

Having belief in yourself

Love and friendship, feeling accepted

Feeling secure and safe in an environment where you are protected

Basic needs such as food, water, warmth, shelter, and sleep

Teachers, parents, brothers and sisters, and friends can help you to stay healthy and happy.

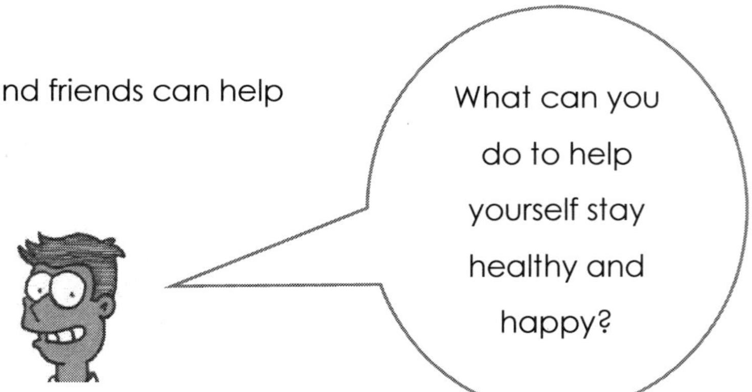

Looking after your physical self

There are 6 things that you can do to help yourself:

Don't play computer games in bed or watch videos. It isn't helpful to listen to loud music. Reading is good but not if it keeps you awake until late at night – no matter how interesting the book is!

Do something active. You may not like sports but you should at least go out for a walk once a week (preferably once a day). Take the dog, if you have one. Get off the bus one stop earlier and walk the rest of the way to school.

Refresh your bedroom. Open your curtains, open the window, let in some fresh air. Check your bedroom for dirty plates and used cups. Hang up your clothes or put them in the wash, and throw away any rubbish.

Keep yourself clean and smelling good. In the morning: Have a shower, but if you don't you should at least wash your face and then brush or comb your hair. Brush your teeth. Use a deodorant under your arms before you put your clothes on. Make sure your underwear is clean. **In the evening:** Have a bath or shower and wash your hair if you didn't do so in the morning. Brush your teeth.

Look after your clothes. Put on clean underwear every day. If your uniform is dirty, put your clothes in the dirty laundry basket, or take them downstairs and put them in the washing machine. Get out a clean shirt / trousers / skirt for the next day.

Go to bed at a reasonable time so that you wake up feeling refreshed and ready for a new day. If you are having trouble getting to sleep because you are worried or anxious, tell someone at home. You could try listening to some slow, quiet music or some gentle water sounds.

Safe spaces and time out places

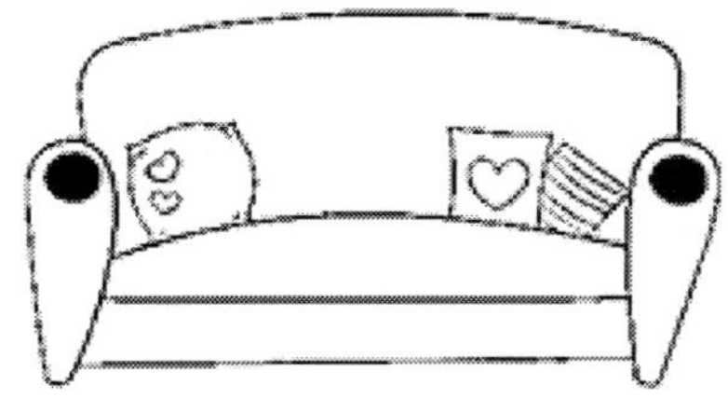

If you are upset by noises or smells, or if you find it stressful to deal with crowds of people, you may need a quiet and calming place in school where you can go to spend some time alone. Perhaps you get tired very easily and need a break during the day.

If you feel anxious or worried, you may need to know that there is a room that you can go to at any time of the school day, and someone that you can talk to – a 'go to' person - about how you are feeling. This might be a teacher, the school nurse, or someone who works in the school office. Your new school needs to know that you may find these things difficult, and you should talk to your parents or carer about finding a safe time out space and 'go to' person.

There is a time out or safe space in my new school in:

The 'go to' person or people in my new school:

Being mindful

It's important to talk about how you are feeling. Everyone gets fed up now and again, but if you are feeling anxious, sad, unhappy or under pressure, it helps to talk about these feelings with someone close to you, perhaps an older brother or sister if you have one, or your parents or carer. Very often, sharing your feelings can make things seem a lot better. This is especially important if you feel that schoolwork is becoming difficult to manage, or if you having trouble with other students or people at school. If there is a problem when you are in school, that needs to be sorted out RIGHT NOW, talk to your class teacher about it. If you work with a Special Needs Assistant, ask them to help you.

Know your strengths

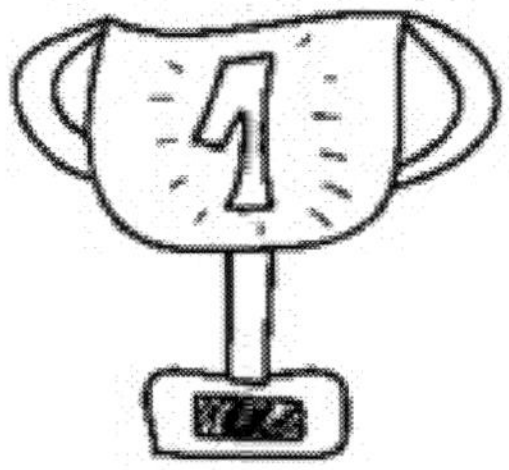

No-one is perfect but everyone is good at something. Some people are good at talking, and others are good listeners. Some people in your school are good at PE and sport, and some are better at drawing or playing an instrument. Some people are good at learning facts, and others are good at having ideas or making plans.

Knowing what you are good at will help you to feel good about yourself, even when you are finding some things in school quite difficult. It can also help you to find a different way of doing things. Take some time to think about your strengths and skills. Practice talking about these and how they might help you to manage the tasks, roles, and routines that you will have in your new school.

Things that I am good at:

Making Friends and Talking to People

At secondary school, there will be many more students than in primary school, and not everyone will have moved from the same school. Some people will already know each other, but other people will not. So everyone will need to make new friends.

It can be difficult to get to know someone new, so it helps to practice meeting new people and introducing yourself. You can practice at home with your family. Sometimes it is useful to video this and play it back, so that you can spot any errors and correct them. However, it is NOT a good idea to record yourself on your mobile phone, or send the video to other people, or upload it to social media, or to YouTube.

Starting a conversation

You can use the script below to help you practice.

Say: "**Hello**" and smile.

Start the conversation by introducing yourself and asking a question: "**I'm John, what's your name?**"

You can continue the conversation by asking about the other person:

- What class are you in? Who is your class teacher?
- Do you have any friends in school?
- Where do you live?

Do not ask about things that might make the other person upset, or which might make them feel, look or sound different. So, for example, don't ask or make any comment about:

- Someone's personal appearance (e.g. hair, skin, clothes)
- The way someone speaks or laughs.

You should talk about this and practice with people at home. Try and think of some more things that you could say to begin a conversation. You could start a conversation with someone in the class or at break or lunch time by saying some of these things:

Conversation rules

Making or having a conversation also follows a set of rules. These are not written down but you have to know and understand how to use them. Join the conversation, or start a new one? How are you going to say it?

Remember. People take turns to talk and listen to each other. You can also ask a question if you don't understand something or to keep the conversation going. At the end of a conversation say "good-bye", "see you later", or "have a nice day."

Watch and listen. Look at what people in the group are doing. Listen to what they are saying. Are they telling stories, joking around, or are they having an argument? Look at their 'body language'.

A good way of remembering this is to **TAP** into the conversation: **Think, Act, Plan**.

Think about what the other person is saying. Is it a story, are they telling a joke? Are they asking a real question, or a [rhetorical] question that doesn't really need an answer?

Act by facing the person who is speaking to you, look at them directly in the face. Try not to look bored or disinterested. Don't stand too close to the other person. Try not to interrupt when they are speaking.

Plan by thinking about what you are going to say. Do you need to carry on the topic of the conversation, or start a new one? What are you going to say?

Joining in with a conversation when two people or a group of people are talking to each other, can be tricky to get right. You need to use your **TAP** skills and figure out when you can join in, and what to say.

Practice your TAP skills. It is helpful to have an idea of some of the things that might come up. You will not have to say all of these things in one conversation, but you might be asked about places that you have been to, summer holidays, where you live, things that you like or dislike. It's useful to think about your answer to some common questions, for example:

I live in ____

I really don't like ______________________________________

I like going to ____

My favourite activity is __________________________________

My favourite computer game is _____________________________

This summer we went to __________________________________

I like reading things like _________________________________

My hobby is ____

Sharing information about yourself

When people have conversations they share information, talk about their feelings, tell a story about something that happened to them, or ask for help with a problem. Talking to people in your family about these things, is quite different to sharing this information with people that you don't know very well. Some people may share the things that you tell them with other students in your school. If you share a secret or information about someone else, you might get into trouble.

Think about the following situations, and think about who you can share this information with, and when you should keep this to yourself. Talk about this with people at home.

- You need to bring a toy or other personal belonging to school with you, so that you feel calm.
- You don't like the person you sit next to in class.
- You got the best mark in class for Maths.
- You have not done your homework.
- You hate tomatoes.

What other things might you want to share?

Sharing information about other people

Sometimes friends will tell you stories about other people or share information about themselves. You should think carefully about whether it is OK to tell other people, but you should not share personal information about what your friend or people in your group or class think about other students, for example:

> "Sean thinks that you are a waste of space. He said so yesterday."

This could get you into all sorts of trouble. You should not share secrets with other people, especially if your friend asked you not to tell anyone else. For example:

> "Tracy said she's scared of the dark and she has to leave the light on at night."

Before you share something that someone has said to you, you should think carefully about:

- How your friend will feel if you share this secret.
- Perhaps they might be teased if other people find out.
- Whether they will be angry or upset with you.

Teasing and Bullying

When people who are friends with you make fun of you in a jokey way, it's called teasing. You might be used to this at home if you have brothers and sisters. Sometimes teasing can go too far or get out of control, and it can be upsetting or hurt people's feelings. If you see someone becoming upset, you should stop teasing them. Before you tease someone by making a joke about something they do or say, or how they look, ask yourself these questions:

- How would I feel if someone said this to me?
- Will they understand that I'm teasing?
- Is it something that they might misunderstand?
- Do I tease people a lot and are they getting fed up with it?

Teasing is not the same as bullying, although if it gets out of hand and becomes more frequent and unpleasant, it might lead to a more serious situation. If someone teases you and the things that they say are very hurtful, or they just won't stop, it's not a good idea to punch them, shout, swear, or call them names. Here are some things that you could do:

1. Ask them to stop.
2. Saying something like:

   "I get the joke but can we move on to something else?"
   "OK very funny, but that's enough now."

3. Ignore the comment, say "OK, I'll talk to you later," and walk away.
4. You could reply by making a sort of jokey comment, for example:

   "Yawn. I've heard that one before."

Bullying

Bullying is more aggressive, unkind or frightening than teasing. It happens when someone deliberately hurts another student, or threatens to hurt them. Bullying happens when someone is:

- Pushed, hit, or tripped on purpose.
- Called names, insulted, or shouted at.
- Threatened or made to feel unsafe.
- Saying or writing nasty things about someone.

A bully might force another student to give them money or their belongings, or force them to do something against their will. Other kinds of bullying happen when a student is not allowed to join in with an activity, or is left out, or is ignored by everyone. If these kinds of things are happening **all of the time**, that is called bullying.

There are some practical things that you can do to stop another student from bullying you, or bullying one of your friends. It's also important that you have a conversation with yourself about what is happening. You can do this by telling yourself that:

- It is not your fault.
- You are not a horrible person.
- Everyone is different and people should accept this.
- Bullying is not acceptable and you do not have to put up with it.

Take action:

- Ignore the people who are bullying you.
- Stay out of their way.
- Keep calm, take a deep breath, think of something else.
- Be confident: stand up / sit up straight, look them in the eye, use a strong voice.

Tell someone.

Talk to a teacher and someone at home if this is happening to you in school.

Personal space

When we talk, work, and play with other people we do this in a space that we share, for example, in a classroom, a playground, or in someone's house. Sometimes we have to share a physical space with other people when we go shopping or use a lift. At home, we share a physical space with other members of our family.

We also have our own personal space, which is an area of space around our bodies that we do not like other people to move into, unless we tell them that it is OK. To find out where your personal space is, stand with your arms out to either side of you. From your body to your fingertips is the personal space that belongs to you.

It is normal for family and very good friends to move into this space, perhaps to give you a hug. Sometimes you might feel uncomfortable if people come too close to you, especially if you do not know them very well. In the same way, you should be careful not to move into another person's space when you are talking to them. Some useful rules to help you think about personal space are:

- Don't stand too close to someone when you are talking to them. You should stay about one arm's length away unless they tell you it is OK to go closer.
- You should not touch other people when you are talking to them, unless they are a member of your family or they say that it is OK for you to do this.
- Sometimes it is OK to be closer than one arm's length to a person, for example when you are in a crowded bus or a lift, when the other person is a close friend or family member, when you are playing a sport or a game.

Managing Tricky Situations

Sometimes things happen in school that might make you upset or anxious. This happens to ALL students, even those who seem to be very confident. If you have a system or strategy or routine to solve problems, very often things can be sorted out quite easily. You might want to try the **7 Steps Problem Sorter**.

1. **Do not panic.** Take a deep breath and say: "If I stay calm, I can solve this problem." Say it aloud, in a firm, clear voice. Sometimes it helps to do this in front of a mirror. Say it again.

2. **WHO is creating the problem?** Think about this carefully.

   Is it a problem caused by a single person or more than one person? Are you one of those people? Do you need to look at your own actions or behaviour?

3. **WHY is the problem, a problem?**

   Are you upset or annoyed because you were prevented from doing something you wanted, needed or had planned to do? Are you upset because someone hurt you or your feelings? Are you worried because something has gone wrong?

4. **HOW can the problem be solved?**

   What could you do or say to fix the problem? Who do you need to speak to? Write down a plan of action.

5. **WHAT might happen next if you follow your plan of action?**

   What are the possible reactions and outcomes?

6. **WHEN could you activate your plan, and do you need anyone to help you?**

7. **CHOOSE the best solution.**

The **7 Steps Problem Sorter** works best when you use it with a partner, for example, a good friend, an older brother or sister, your parents or guardians, or someone else at home. It's a very good idea to practice this in the school holidays, before you move to your new secondary school.

Talk with a friend or someone at home about how you could solve the following problems, and use the **7SPS** to help you:

1. You see a student being pushed around.

2. You see another student crying in the corridor.

3. You think you have lost your mobile phone in school.

4. You see a student taking something from another student's school bag.

5. You find someone's purse, wallet, or bus pass in the changing rooms.

6. You have had an accident with your uniform.

7. You have forgotten to bring your lunch.

8. You cannot find your way to a classroom.

9. You have missed the bus to / from school.

10. Your best friend ignored you at school today.

Using Situation Cards

Sometimes when things go wrong at school the situation can make you become anxious or even panic. Perhaps you forgot to do your homework, or bring your PE kit. Maybe your friend is not speaking to you, or is spending time with other people.

Situation Cards can help you to decide what you should do. Think about three 'what if' situations about school, or travelling to school:

1. ______________________________

2. ______________________________

3. ______________________________

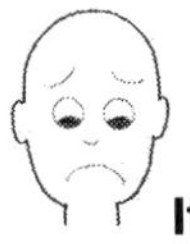

If I am feeling unwell and need to leave the classroom

1. Raise my hand to get the teacher's attention.
2. Wait for my teacher to say my name.
3. Say "I don't feel well, please may I leave the room?"
4. Go to the bathroom first if I need to.
5. Go to Mrs. White in room B4 on the second floor.

EVERYONE (even your teacher and your parents) remembers what it was like when things went wrong at school. This is an example of a Situation Card which would help you to make a decision if you felt unwell in school.

Once you know the names of the teachers and the rooms in your new school, you can make Situation Cards. You can ask someone at home to help you. You can cover the cards in plastic and keep them in your school bag. Not everything that happens unexpectedly at school needs a Situation Card. Work out a solution for the following situations:

- You don't know where to go for your next lesson.
- You forgot to write down the homework.
- You have lost the key to your locker.
- You have forgotten your pencil case.

Friends. Ask friends or other students if you don't know where to go or what to do. They can also help you with finding your way to places in school. You can ask them what homework needs to be done if you are not certain or cannot remember.

Teachers. Ask your teachers if you don't know what to do in class or for homework. They will also be able to help you if you have forgotten something or don't know where to go.

People at home. People at home will be able to help you plan and organise your equipment and homework. They will want to know if you are having any difficulties. They will be able to help you work out the best plan of action, and the best person to go to in school.

Most of the time it is easier just to ask someone that you trust for help or advice.

About Me

Now that we have discovered the important information about your new school, and to manage new situations, we can think about what your new school may need to know about you.

Your teacher might organise this by asking you to create a 'passport' or personal profile to send to your new school, and it will be shared with the teachers before you arrive. Find out if your class teacher is going to do this. If not, you can create your own About Me book and ask your parents to send this to your new school. What would you like to include? What would it be useful for your teacher to know about you? How are you going to give this information to your new teacher?

You could make an information booklet using a blank exercise book, or you could use some blank pieces of paper and staple them together.

Perhaps you enjoy drawing and illustrating comic strips or cartoons, or making short animations.

You could write a poem or even draw a diagram…

To help you think about the sort of information to include in your information file, comic strip or illustrated book, make some brief notes about yourself using the table on the next page. What kind of things are important for your new teachers to know?

Notes About Me
My name and age
People in my family
Where I live
Activities that I enjoy
Pets
Places I like to go
Activities I do not like to do in school
Activities that I like to do in school
Things that I find difficult are
I am really good at
Sometimes I worry about
I am allergic to

Congratulations !

You have reached the end of this workbook. I hope that you have found the activities useful, and that it has given you more confidence about going to a new school.

Good luck ....

.... and enjoy yourself

Printed in Great Britain
by Amazon

42246604R00046